20th Century
PERSPECTIVES

The Harlem Renaissance

Adam R. Schaefer

Heinemann Library
Chicago, Illinois

© 2003 Heinemann Library
a division of Reed Elsevier Inc.
Chicago, Illinois

Customer Service 888-454-2279
Visit our website at www.heinemannlibrary.com

Produced for Heinemann Library by Discovery Books
Designed by Barry Dwyer
Consultant: Andrew Frank
Originated by QueNet
Printed and bound the United States by Lake Book Manufacturing, Inc.

07 06 05 04 03
10 9 8 7 6 5 4 3 2 1

Library of Congress Cataloging-in-Publication Data
Schaefer, A. R. (Adam Richard), 1976-
  The Harlem Renaissance / Adam R. Schaefer.
    p. cm. -- (20th-century perspectives)
Summary: Describes the time period known as the Harlem Renaissance, during which African American artists, poets, writers, thinkers, and musicians flourished in Harlem, New York.
Includes bibliographical references and index.
  ISBN 1-4034-0150-0 (hardcover)   ISBN 1-4034-3858-7 (paperback)
  1. African Americans--Intellectual life--20th century--Juvenile literature. 2. Harlem Renaissance--Juvenile literature. 3. African Americans--History--1877-1964--Juvenile literature. 4. African American arts--History--20th century--Juvenile literature. 5. Harlem (New York, N.Y.)--Intellectual life--20th century--Juvenile literature. 6. African American intellectuals--New York (State)--New York--History--20th century--Juvenile literature. [1. Harlem Renaissance. 2. African Americans--History--1877-1964. 3. African American arts. 4. Harlem (New York, N.Y.)--History.] I. Title. II. Series.
  E185.6 .S35 2002
                                        2002006383

Acknowledgments
The author and publishers are grateful to the following for permission to reproduce copyright material: Bettmann/Corbis pp. 23, 35, 41; Bridgeman Art Library p. 31; Christie's Images/Corbis p. 33; Ciniglio Lorenzo/Corbis Sygma p. 42; Corbis pp. 21, 22, 24, 39; Hulton Archive pp. 4, 5, 13, 18, 25, 27, 29, 36, 38; Lucien Aigner/Corbis p. 40; Peter Newark's American Pictures pp. 7, 8, 12, 26, 28; Schomburg Collection pp. 11, 14, 16, 20, 30, 32 (photograph copyright Morgan and Marvin Smith); Underwood & Underwood/Corbis pp. 15, 37.

Cover photograph reproduced with permission of Bettmann/Corbis.

Every effort has been made to contact copyright holders of any material reproduced in this book. Any omissions will be rectified in subsequent printings if notice is given to the publisher.

Some words are shown in bold, **like this.** You can find out what they mean by looking in the glossary.

Contents

What Was the Harlem Renaissance?

In the 1920s and early 1930s, a part of New York City called Harlem became the center of an African-American artistic, political, and social movement known as the Harlem Renaissance. During this time, Harlem became known for its outstanding black writers, thinkers, poets, musicians, leaders, and artists. The word Renaissance, which in French means "rebirth," was used to show the sudden advancement of culture and the arts in Harlem. The original cultural Renaissance took place in Europe between the 13th and 15th centuries.

Harlem is a two-square-mile area of New York City on the northern end of Manhattan Island. Native Americans lived in the area for thousands of years before Dutch settlers began moving there in the early 17th century. When the first settlers arrived, Harlem was several miles away from New York City (known as New Amsterdam at the time). Over time, the city grew closer to Harlem, and Harlem eventually became part of New York City.

The Great Migration

For much of the 19th century, Harlem was inhabited by Irish, Italian, and Jewish immigrants. That changed at the beginning of the 20th century. Social pressures in the South drove large numbers of African Americans to northern cities, including New York, in search of jobs. This movement of people became known as the Great Migration. Harlem was an affordable place for many African Americans to live. The onset of World War One meant that there were many jobs to be had, drawing even more blacks to Harlem.

On July 28, 1917, the NAACP organized a silent parade in New York City to protest violence in East St. Louis, Illinois, Memphis, Tennessee, and Waco, Texas. The founding of groups such as the NAACP and the National Urban League was important to the success of the Harlem Renaissance.

Race riots and other social factors led African Americans to become organized through groups like the National Association for the Advancement of Colored People (**NAACP**) and the **National Urban League**. These groups worked to bring rights to black people throughout the country. Black leaders such as W. E. B. DuBois and Charles S. Johnson recognized the talent that existed in Harlem and in the black community as a whole. They promoted promising artists, writers, and musicians, connecting them with white publishers and **patrons**.

A cultural awakening

These creative people fed off of each other's energy, and many of them were talented in more than one area. Poets wrote musicals, authors painted and drew, musicians danced and wrote. As the movement grew, more and more black people were drawn to the area. Harlem became the center of black culture in the United States. And, for the first time in the history of the United States, black art, literature, and music were taken seriously by a large number of whites.

Fletcher Henderson's Orchestra was one of the first large bands to play jazz music. The famous trumpet player Louis Armstrong is in the middle of the back row in this photo from 1924.

While the United States was going through a difficult time in race relations, Harlem was mostly immune to these problems, after the late 1910s. This made Harlem a safe destination for many blacks. It was one of the few truly African-American locales in the country, a place where the culture, arts, and institutions of black people were the rule, instead of the exception.

The end of an era

In the early 1930s, several factors came together to end the Harlem Renaissance. The **stock market** crash in 1929 caused many people to lose their jobs, making luxuries like the arts unaffordable. As artists, writers, and musicians became well known, they had the money to travel. Many took jobs in education in other parts of the country.

Still, the Harlem Renaissance had long-lasting effects that are felt even today. Many doors were opened to black artists and writers for the first time. A **legacy** of success in the art, music, and publishing worlds was established, paving the way for future generations to be successful as well.

Early Harlem

Historians aren't sure when the first European saw Manhattan Island. Some think that it might have been as early as the first decade of the 1500s. The first confirmed sighting was in 1524. Italian Giovanni da Verrazzano was piloting a ship for the French government. Verrazzano and his crew were looking for a shortcut from Europe to China and Japan. When he and his men entered New York Harbor, boats full of Native Americans greeted them. The local Indians were friendly and cheerful, but a storm forced Verrazzano and his crew back into the open ocean. During the next 75 years, many European fur traders explored the area and traded with the Lenape Indians. The French, English, Dutch, Spanish, and Portuguese all had explorers or traders in the New York Harbor area during this time.

The first Dutch

In 1609, Henry Hudson, an English explorer working for the Dutch, sailed up the river on the west side of Manhattan Island. He went all the way to what is now Albany, New York. Later, the river was named for him, and it is still called the Hudson River. Like other explorers, Hudson was trying to find a shortcut to eastern Asia. He didn't find it, but he was impressed with the area. There was great farming land, a wealth of birds, rivers loaded with fish, and all kinds of wildlife on land. The local Indians also seemed to be friendly. After hearing about the island's natural resources, in 1621 the Dutch government gave the Dutch West India Company permission to establish colonies in the area. The company sent settlers to different parts of present-day New York and New Jersey.

Buying Manhattan

In 1626, the Dutch West India Company tricked the Lenape Indians into selling the island of Manhattan. The Company paid 60 Dutch guilders for the island—about $24—and began building a fort and planning a settlement that the Dutch called Nieuw (New) Amsterdam. The Indians remained the majority on Manhattan Island for another hundred years.

In 1648, Petrus Stuyvesant became the governor of Nieuw Amsterdam. He was interested in building more settlements in the surrounding areas. In 1658, he offered residents of Nieuw Amsterdam the chance to own large blocks of land in a new settlement called Nieuw Haarlem. The area was north of Nieuw Amsterdam on Manhattan Island in a hilly, swampy area. Nieuw Haarlem was named for Haarlem, a Dutch city.

Beginnings of Harlem

New residents were offered 40 to 50 acres (16 to 20 hectares) of land and protection from thieves and Indians. Immigrants from many different countries settled the area. In the first few years, French, Danes, Swedes, Germans, Dutch, and **Walloons** all moved to Nieuw Haarlem. Only a wagon road connected the town with Nieuw Amsterdam. Most people took a boat from the lower tip of Manhattan to get up to Nieuw Haarlem.

In 1664, Charles II, the King of England, gave all of the Dutch holdings in this area to his brother, the Duke of York. England didn't own this land, but that didn't stop Charles II from giving it anyway. The Duke sent troops to the area, and the Dutch leadership gave up the land to the English without any fight.

Name change

When the English took control of Nieuw Amsterdam, they renamed the territory "New York" in honor of the Duke. The English had similar plans for Nieuw Haarlem, but the locals convinced them to drop the Nieuw and use the more English spelling, Harlem. The English were satisfied, and Harlem was the new name of the town.

By 1659, Nieuw Amsterdam was a bustling Dutch city. A few miles to the north, Nieuw Haarlem was just getting started. Just five years later, the city would be claimed by the English and renamed "New York."

Black Manhattan

When rail lines were extended to Harlem in the early 1800s, it made it easier for people to live in Harlem and travel to work in New York City. This New York and Harlem Rail Road timetable is from 1848.

As New York grew, some of the wealthy residents of the city built large estates in Harlem. In the late 18th century, Harlem was a vacation destination for the wealthy. Then, in 1827, it became illegal to own slaves in New York. At first they were replaced by poor servants, but the rich found it increasingly difficult to find enough people to care for their huge mansions. Many of the wealthy left the area.

Getting connected

In the early part of the 19th century, railroads built lines from downtown New York out to Harlem, making it easier for people to get to Harlem. During the middle part of the century, immigrants moved toward Harlem because it cost less to live there. People could live in Harlem and take the train to work in New York. The old estates were taken over and turned into **tenement houses** for the poor. The city authorities flattened the hills and filled in the swamps to make room for more homes. More and more immigrants moved into shacks and old estates, where the living conditions were terrible.

In the late 19th century, the rich whites again moved to Harlem. Conditions weren't good in downtown New York. Prices were high and it was becoming crowded. Real estate developers tore down the Harlem **slums** and built expensive homes and apartments. This made the value of other local properties rise. The area was so attractive, that New York City **annexed** Harlem in 1873. After a while, Harlem property was too expensive for the white working class, and they left the area.

Around 1900, many people were leaving Harlem and the cost of housing went down. The landlords and real estate agents couldn't convince the middle-class whites to move in. They were worried that if they did, prices would rise again.

A solution to two problems

A black **realtor** named Philip A. Payton, Jr. analyzed the problems with the Harlem real estate market and thought of a solution. He knew that

NEW-YORK AND HARLEM RAIL ROAD,
DAILY.
FALL ARRANGEMENT.

On and after **TUESDAY, OCTOBER 10th, 1848,** the Cars will run as follows, until further notice.

TRAINS WILL LEAVE CITY HALL, N. Y., FOR

Harlem & Morrisania	Fordham & William's Bridge.	Hunt's Bridge, Underhill's & Hart's Corners.	Davis' Brook, Pleasantville, Chapequa, Mount Kisko, Bedford, Mechanicsville, Purdy's and Croton Falls.
7 10 A.M. 12 M.			
8 " 2 P.M.	7 A.M. 3 30 P.M.	9 A.M.: 5 30 P.M.	
9 " 3 "	9 " 5 30 "		
10 " 4 "	12 M. 6 30 "	T'kahoe & White Plains:	
5 30 "		7 A.M.: 3 30 P.M.	7 A.M: 3 30 P.M.
6 30 "		9 " 5 30 "	9 " 4 "

NOTICE.

Passengers are reminded of the great danger of standing upon the Platforms of the Cars, and hereby notified that the practice is contrary to the rules of the Company, and that they do not admit any responsibility for injury sustained by any Passenger upon the platforms, in case of accident.

RETURNING TO NEW-YORK, WILL LEAVE

Harlem & Morrisania	Hant's Bridge.	White Plains.	Bedford
7 08 A.M. 1 10 P.M.	7 50 A.M. 3 15 P.M.	7 15 A.M. 2 45 P.M.	7 55 A.M. 1 55 P.M.
8 " 3 "		8 25 " 3 "	4 95 "
8 20 " 3 45 "	Underhill's Road.	Davis' Brook.	Mechanicsville.
9 " 4 "	7 40 A.M. 3 06 P.M.	8 26 A.M. 2 35 P.M.	7 45 A.M. 1 45 P.M.
11 " 5 "		4 55 "	4 15 "
" 6 "	Tackahoe.	Pleasantville.	Purdy's
Fordham & William's Bridge.	7 35 A.M. 3 03 P.M.	8 18 A.M. 2 20 P.M.	7 35 A.M. 1 35 P.M.
	8 50 " 5 15 "	4 48 "	4 05 "
6 45 A.M. 1 15 P.M.		Mount Kisko.	Croton Falls.
8 " 3 25 "	Harts Corners.	8 A.M.: 2 P.M.	7 30 A.M. 1 30 P.M.
9 10 " 5 40 "	7 25 A.M. 2 50 P.M.	4 30 "	4 "

The TRAINS FOR HARLEM & MORRISANIA, leaving City Hall at 7,10, 8, 9, 10, 12, 2, 3, 4, and 6.30. and From Morrisania and Harlem at 7.08, 8, 9, 11, 1.40, 3, 4, 5 and 6, will land and receive Passengers at 27th, 42d, 51st, 61st, 79th, 86th, 109th, 115th, 125th and 132d streets.

The 7 A. M. and 3.30 P. M. Trains from New-York to CROTON FALLS and the 7.30 A. M. Train from Croton Falls will not stop between White Plains and New-York, except at Tuckahoe, William's Bridge and Fordham.

A Car will precede each Train 10 minutes, to take up passengers in the City; the last Car will not stop except at Broome street, and 32nd street

FREIGHT TRAINS leave New-York at 9 A. M. & 12 M.; leave CROTON FALLS at 7 A. M. & 8 P. M.

On SUNDAYS an Extra Train at 1 o'clock P. M. to Harlem and Morrisania.

Nesbitt, Printer.

the landlords and real estate agents needed to find tenants. He also knew that many blacks living in lower Manhattan were looking for better housing.

Payton negotiated with some of the white landlords in the area. He found middle-class black families to move into Harlem and rent their properties. However, when Payton started trying to move families west of Lenox Avenue the white upper-class there didn't want to have black people as neighbors. They bought up houses and buildings and evicted the black residents.

Fighting back

Payton and other black business owners were upset that upper-class whites were keeping black people from good housing. They decided to "fight fire with fire" and formed the Afro-American Realty Company. The company began purchasing homes and apartment buildings west of Lenox Avenue. They evicted the white tenants and rented to black families. This was successful for a while, but eventually whites convinced the banks and **mortgage** holders not to lend money to blacks in Harlem. This didn't stop Payton. He started using his own money to purchase homes and buildings and renting them to blacks.

In 1911, the St. Philip's Episcopal Church—the biggest black church in New York—moved to Harlem and built a new church. Then the church bought a row of 13 apartment buildings on 135th Street and rented them to black residents. Soon, more and more black churches and social clubs were moving to the area. Just a few years after St. Philip's moved to Harlem, the culture had changed so much that people started calling it "Black Manhattan" and "Negro City in New York."

Payton's profits

Philip A. Payton, Jr. describing his success in the Harlem real estate market:

"One fine day I made a deal that netted me nearly $1150 . . . From that time things grew better . . . I bought the flat house [apartment] in which I was living. I bought two more flats and kept them five months when I sold them at a profit of $5000. I bought another, kept it a month, and made $2750, another and made $1500, another and made $2600, and so on. In all I have owned from time to time nine five-story flats and five private houses."

The Economy Grows

Even though more and more black people were moving to Harlem, the business opportunities there weren't as great as they were in lower Manhattan. Many people took the train to work in other parts of New York, but that was slow until the Lenox Avenue subway line was built in 1904. After the subway was completed, residents of Harlem could get to jobs in other parts of the city much more quickly.

Limited success

A few black business owners, such as Philip A. Payton, Jr., T. C. Thomas, and J. B. Nail, were making money by dealing in Harlem real estate, but, at first, there weren't many other business opportunities for black residents. Much of that changed during the 1910s.

When World War One broke out, many new European immigrants went back to their homelands to fight. After the United States got involved in 1917, many more residents were called to arms. This freed up thousands of jobs in New York City. Suddenly, Harlem blacks were finding jobs all over New York. The local economy was booming. The word spread throughout the country and hundreds of thousands of Southern blacks moved to Northern cities to get away from **segregation**, **Jim Crow laws**, and a poor economy. Many had lived in towns and cities and were well educated with useful skills to offer.

The self-made millionaire

Madam C. J. Walker was the first female **self-made millionaire** in the United States. She grew up poor, but developed her own line of hair care products for blacks. She went door-to-door throughout the South for years before settling in Indianapolis in 1910. There, Walker built a

Pig Foot Mary

One of the most colorful **entrepreneurs** in Harlem was Lillian Harris. Harris was born in the South in 1870. In 1901, she moved to New York. When she arrived, Lillian had five dollars with her. She spent three dollars on an old baby carriage and a boiler, and another two dollars on pigs' feet. She set up the baby carriage as a portable food stand and sold her pigs' feet to other relocated Southern blacks. Soon, she began selling all kinds of Southern food, and traded in the baby carriage for a steam table. Everyone in Harlem knew the woman at the corner of 135th and Lenox Avenue as "Pig Foot Mary." Later in life she became wealthy by investing in real estate.

factory, a salon, and a training school. Walker's daughter, A'Lelia, heard about what was happening in Harlem, and in 1913, she moved there. Walker herself moved to Harlem in 1916. She opened an office there and ran her factory from New York.

Getting involved

Walker got very involved with the community in Harlem. She gave money to black organizations and was particularly involved in social justice. After more than 30 blacks were murdered by a white mob in Illinois, Walker and other local leaders went to Washington, D.C., to pressure the government to do more to stop **lynchings**.

Walker was also interested in helping black women succeed. She trained beauticians and hair stylists at her schools and had a large network of women that used and sold her products. Walker held a national meeting of her **agents** in Philadelphia in 1917. Many historians believe that it was the first large gathering of businesswomen in the United States.

Walker's **legacy** is enormous. In her lifetime, she turned $1.25 of her own money into a million-dollar business. She was also a **philanthropist** who gave away large sums of money to historically black universities, and to social organizations designed to help black people. After her death, her daughter, A'Lelia, continued in the tradition and supported and promoted black artists and writers in Harlem.

Madam C. J. Walker (driving car) was one of the first black women to own an automobile and the first female self-made millionaire in the United States. She began selling her products in the Southern U.S. before moving to Indianapolis and then Harlem in 1916.

11

City of Refuge

As more and more people moved to Harlem, businesses and opportunities followed them: hairdressers and barbershops, restaurants and social clubs, nightclubs and churches. Many Southern blacks found the conditions attractive in Harlem. They had most of the comforts of their Southern homes without **segregation** and **Jim Crow laws**.

Still, things weren't perfect in Harlem. Black residents faced **discrimination** from local whites. Some whites formed groups that tried to keep blacks from moving into certain neighborhoods. Some even talked about building a 24-foot- (7-meter-) tall fence to keep blacks out of their area.

Preaching self-reliance

A man named Marcus Garvey moved to Harlem in 1916. Garvey was born in Jamaica, but had lived in several different countries, including London, England. Before he moved to New York he started a group in Jamaica called the Universal Negro Improvement Association (**UNIA**). UNIA set up branches in many different cities and countries. The headquarters was moved from Jamaica to Harlem in 1916.

Marcus Garvey (seated behind driver) started the Universal Negro Improvement Association in Jamaica. When Garvey moved to Harlem in 1916, he moved the UNIA headquarters there, too. Here, Garvey drives through Harlem in 1924.

Garvey wanted black communities to become self-reliant. He wanted black people to spend money in black businesses. Many blacks liked Garvey's ideas, but some thought he was too **radical**. Garvey's thoughts angered some white people. They didn't like the idea of blacks becoming **self-sufficient**. And when blacks took many of the jobs left by white soldiers who went to fight in World War One, it angered a few whites to the point of violence.

The Red Summer

During the summer of 1917, things got out of control in East St. Louis, Illinois. East St. Louis was a primarily black suburb of St. Louis, Missouri. In July, some whites drove through the town firing shots into the homes of blacks. Black residents shot and killed two policemen that they mistakenly thought were responsible. This resulted in a full-scale riot. Whites burned down black houses and apartment buildings. People who tried to escape from the fires were killed when they left their buildings. At least 39 people died during the riots.

During the "Red Summer" of 1919, race riots broke out in cities all over the United States. Here, the National Guard was called out to help control the riot in Chicago in July.

After World War One, many white and immigrant men returned home to find things much different than when they left. In their absence, blacks had taken their jobs and moved into their neighborhoods. During the summer of 1919, in cities across the United States, whites attacked blacks, starting **race riots**. Members of the **Ku Klux Klan** provoked many of the attacks. Klansmen terrorized many minority groups, but especially blacks. They would often ride on horses, burning black homes while hidden beneath white robes and hoods. That summer, more than 60 black citizens were **lynched** in cities from New Orleans to Chicago to New York. The bloodshed earned the hot months of 1919 the nickname "Red Summer."

Although there were still conflicts with white neighbors, African Americans living in Harlem during this time had a much better life than blacks in most other parts of the United States.

The Struggle for Racial Justice

In the South, the political and social institutions in place didn't allow African Americans to form organizations. As large segments of the black population moved north to the big cities, people found the freedom to unite and push political and social **agendas**.

Getting organized

Garvey's **UNIA** was one organization that pressed for change. Another was the National Association for the Advancement of Colored People (**NAACP**). The NAACP was started in 1909 in Illinois after a **race riot**. The group's methods were different from those of the UNIA. Where the UNIA tried to build the black community from within, promoting self-reliance, the NAACP actively campaigned for equal treatment using established political channels. The group filed lawsuits, represented black defendants in criminal trials, and pressured **legislators** to enact **civil rights** laws. In other words, they demanded equal treatment using historically white institutions.

During 1919, the year of the Red Summer, the NAACP focused on the problem of **lynchings** in the United States. The group held a conference on lynching and began pressuring U.S. Congressmen and Senators to pass a federal law outlawing lynching. Of course, murder was against the law in all parts of the country, but in some parts of the United States, whites were rarely prosecuted—or found guilty—in the murders of black people. The NAACP hoped that a federal law would make sure that no lynching went unpunished. Eventually, a bill came to the U.S. Senate, but it did not pass. Another attempt was made in the 1930s to pass anti-lynching legislation, but again, nothing became law. Lynchings continued on a regular basis, especially in the South, through the 1950s.

The Committee on Urban Conditions Among Negroes was another group organized to help the advancement of black people. The group was formed in 1910 to help Southern blacks relocate to northern cities. Although the Committee began in New York, it quickly spread to 30 other cities. In 1920, the group shortened its name to the **National Urban League**.

The NAACP was founded in 1909 and began publishing The Crisis a year later. This May 1923 issue features a painting by Laura Wheeler Waring, a popular artist of the era.

The CRISIS

APRIL 1923   15 cents the copy

Giving a voice

Both the NAACP and the National Urban League produced important publications that educated and entertained people, as well as advanced the groups' causes. The NAACP brought out *The Crisis*, in 1910. Each month's issue had **editorials** and essays that pushed the group's viewpoint, but it also included poetry and fiction from black writers that had never been published before. It also featured cover illustrations or drawings from black artists.

In 1923, the National Urban League published the first issue of *Opportunity: A Journal of Negro Life*. Like *The Crisis*, *Opportunity* discussed relevant issues of the day while giving aspiring writers and artists their first chances at publication. These two publications were run by some of the most respected leaders in the black community. W. E. B. DuBois was the first editor-in-chief of *The Crisis*, while Charles S. Johnson edited *Opportunity*.

This parade down 7th Avenue in Harlem was part of the opening ceremonies for the First International Convention of the Negro Peoples of the World.

Major events

The groups also organized large events. The UNIA held the First International Convention of the Negro Peoples of the World in 1920 at Madison Square Garden in midtown Manhattan. DuBois led several **Pan-African Congress** meetings. The presence of these groups and intellectuals in Harlem had an effect in drawing other thinkers to the area. James Weldon Johnson, Alain Locke, and Walter White were just a few of the people who moved to Harlem to contribute to the movement. Locke became famous for editing *The New Negro*, a magazine issue, and later a book, that featured several prominent writers. White was secretary of the NAACP for a time. He also wrote several novels featuring race and lynchings as themes.

The Intellectual Heavyweights

Many men and women had an effect on what was happening in Harlem, but W. E. B. DuBois and Charles S. Johnson were two of the most influential. They were leaders in powerful organizations and editors of two of the most important publications of the time.

A man of conviction

DuBois was born in Great Barrington, Massachusetts. He was very intelligent and left high school early. He had hoped to attend Harvard University, but his mother made arrangements for him to attend Fisk University, a black college in Nashville, Tennessee. After receiving his **bachelor's degree** at Fisk, he studied at the University of Berlin, in Germany, and then was accepted into graduate studies at Harvard. He became the first African American to earn a graduate degree at Harvard.

After he left Harvard, DuBois taught at several universities and traveled throughout many foreign countries. As a result of his experiences, he felt it was important to bring black people from around the world together. This belief is called Pan-Africanism. DuBois helped organize the first **Pan-African Congress** in 1900. In 1905, DuBois met with other black leaders in the Buffalo, New York, area. The group of about 30 decided that the black movement needed to be stronger. At that time, Booker T. Washington was very popular among African Americans. Washington favored a policy of "accommodation." He thought that blacks should try to get along with whites and gain acceptance. DuBois and the other leaders disagreed. They felt that blacks needed to demand their rights and use every legal remedy to get them. The result of those meetings near Buffalo was the Niagara Movement, one of the first **civil rights** movements in the United States. The movement merged into the **NAACP** a few years later in Illinois. DuBois was a leader in the NAACP for most of his life.

A scholar and thinker

Charles S. Johnson was born in Bristol, Virginia, in 1893. He grew up in a middle-class family and was well read and educated as a youth. He studied and graduated from Virginia Union University before earning a graduate degree at the University of Chicago. While in Chicago, Johnson began working for the **National Urban League** office there. His work was interrupted when he enlisted in the army during World War One and was shipped to France.

He returned to Chicago in 1919 and resumed his work with the Chicago Urban League. After the Chicago **race riot** that year, Johnson studied the causes and presented a plan to the governor of Illinois. The governor accepted his plan, and appointed Johnson associate executive secretary of Chicago's Commission on Race Relations. Under Johnson's leadership, the commission produced an important report called *The Negro In Chicago*. His work in Chicago got him noticed nationally and, in 1921, he moved to Harlem to take a job with the National Urban League, where Johnson became the national director of research and investigations. Part of his job was to edit *Opportunity: A Journal of Negro Life*. While he was editor, Johnson gave opportunities to many young and promising black writers who would later become famous. Later in life, Johnson spent many years in the education system, eventually becoming the University of Chicago's first black president.

Charles S. Johnson became involved with the civil rights movement with the National Urban League and later as editor of Opportunity magazine.

Talent Meets Opportunity

The powerful people in Harlem during this time felt a responsibility to African Americans that had talent but were going unrecognized. This is one of the reasons that editors like DuBois and Johnson printed stories and poetry from writers that were previously unknown.

The helpful librarian

One of the groundbreaking events of the Harlem Renaissance got its start with a public librarian. Regina M. Andrews was an assistant at the Harlem branch of the New York Public Library. Andrews was very involved with the theater. With writer and artist Gwendolyn Bennett she started the Negro Experimental Theater, a group of black actors and actresses that performed plays written by black playwrights.

Countee Cullen first won a national poetry contest when he was only 20 years old. Two years later, he became famous after he won the Amy Spingarn Award from The Crisis.

Andrews also tried her hand at writing—she wrote a script for a play called *Climbing Jacob's Ladder*. She was friends with several black artists and writers and knew that they had talent, but didn't have anywhere to display it to the general public. Andrews was also active in the **National Urban League** and knew Charles S. Johnson. She encouraged Johnson to bring black writers together with white magazine and book publishers.

Civic Club dinner

Johnson decided to do it, and in March 1924, he held a dinner at the Civic Club in Harlem. The dinner was an opportunity for many talented writers to talk to white publishers. Some publishers realized that there was a large market of untapped talent. Suddenly, African-American writers were published in famous magazines and getting book contracts. Countee Cullen was one writer—a poet—who had not been widely known previously. After the dinner, he was published in several magazines, including *Harper's Magazine, Poetry,* and *Century Magazine.* Later that year, he published his first book of poetry, *Color.*

Other publications quickly followed. In March 1925, a magazine called *Survey Graphic* devoted an entire issue to the works of black writers. Talented writers such as W. E. B. DuBois, Charles S. Johnson, Langston Hughes, Countee Cullen, and James Weldon Johnson were featured in the issue, edited by Alain Locke. It was an incredibly popular issue, and the magazine later published it as a book called *The New Negro.*

Opportunity: A Journal of Negro Life, the National Urban League's publication edited by Charles S. Johnson, and *The Crisis,* edited by DuBois, also helped identify and nurture new talent. The publications held writing and poetry contests and published the winners' works. Several well-known writers got their start, or boosted their careers, by winning these contests.

Influential Harlem

James Weldon Johnson, writing in *The New Negro:*
"175,000 Negroes live closely together in Harlem . . . 75,000 more than live in any Southern city, and do so without any race friction.
"I believe that the Negro's advantages and opportunities are greater in Harlem than in any other place in the country, and that Harlem will become the intellectual, the cultural and the financial center for Negroes of the United States, and will exert a vital influence upon all Negro peoples."

The New Negro

Part of Alain Locke's essay "Enter the New Negro" from *The New Negro:*
"With this renewed self-respect and self-dependence, the life of the Negro community is bound to enter a new dynamic phase. . . The migrant masses, shifting from countryside to city, hurdle several generations of experience at a leap, but more important, the same thing happens spiritually in the life-attitudes and self-expression of the Young Negro, in his poetry, his art, his education and his new outlook."

And the Winners Are . . .

In 1925, both *Opportunity* and *The Crisis* held awards dinners to recognize their contest winners. The *Opportunity* dinner featured several awards for categories such as plays, poetry, short stories, and essays. *Opportunity* received more than 700 entries for the contest.

Langston Hughes won the *Opportunity* poetry contest for his poem "The Weary Blues." The poem was about a blues musician in Harlem, and included a reference to Lenox Avenue. After the awards dinner, a guest introduced Hughes to editors from the publishing house Alfred A. Knopf. A year later, Knopf published Hughes' collection of poetry, also called *The Weary Blues*.

Other winners

Countee Cullen won second prize for his poem, "To One Who Said Me Nay." The award was one of many that Cullen would win that year. He would later become an assistant editor for *Opportunity*.

E. Franklin Frazier was another winner. He won for an essay on social equality. At the time, Frazier was a **sociology** instructor in Atlanta. In 1927, he wrote an essay linking racial prejudice and insanity. At the

Many people threw parties for artists and writers during the Harlem Renaissance. From left to right, Langston Hughes, Charles S. Johnson, E. Franklin Frazier, Rudolph Fisher and politician Hubert Delaney attend a party in honor of Hughes.

time, Atlanta was a city with a very deep racial divide. Frazier was forced to leave town after his essay was published. He went on to have a successful academic career and is best known for his writing about black families in the United States. He published several books on the subject, including *Black Bourgeoisie* in 1957.

Zora Neale Hurston won two second place awards at the dinner: for a short story called "Spunk" and a play, *Color Struck*. The characters in "Spunk" do most of the narration, talking in a local **dialect**. The story was about a murder in a small town in Florida, and the suspicious death of the murderer that follows. The play *Color Struck* was about the **discrimination** that existed within the black community toward people—especially women—that were too dark or too light.

Amy Spingarn Award

The Crisis had its own honor— the Amy Spingarn Award. In 1925 *The Crisis* received nearly 600 entries. Many of the winners of the *Opportunity* award also won the Spingarn award. Cullen won a prize for a different poem, "Two Moods of Love." Hughes won second prize in the essays division for "The Fascination of Cities," and third prize for "Poems." Not all award winners came from New York. Rudolph Fisher, a doctor from Washington, D.C., won first prize for his story, "High Yaller." Marita Bonner, another resident of Washington, won for her essay, "On Being Young, a Woman, and Colored."

These contests gave exposure to writers that many hadn't heard of before. As a direct result of winning awards, African-American writers made names for themselves throughout the white publishing world.

Zora Neale Hurston became well known for her use of authentic dialects in her works. Hurston explored racial issues in her plays and short stories.

A Wealth of Interesting Writers

Through writing contests, organized dinners, and other arrangements, African-American writers were better known than at any previous time in American history. These writers covered a variety of **genres**, from short story to novel to non-fiction to play to poem and everything in between. The voices that told these stories were also very different. Some writers used **dialects**, others wrote using formal English.

Poet, author, and songwriter

James Weldon Johnson is best known for his poetry, but it was his novel, *The Autobiography of an Ex-Colored Man*, that first garnered attention in the writing world. Johnson was born in 1871 in Jacksonville, Florida. After he graduated from the University of Atlanta, he became a high school principal in his hometown. Johnson was interested in music and songwriting, and in 1900, he wrote the lyrics to a song called "Lift Every Voice and Sing." The song became very popular in the black community and came to be known as the "Negro National Anthem." The next year, Johnson moved to New York City to write songs with his brother.

James Weldon Johnson was born and educated in the South. He first gained attention with his novel, The Autobiography of an Ex-Colored Man.

In 1912, Johnson's book, *The Autobiography of an Ex-Colored Man*, was published. The novel is about a black musician who passes as a white man in order to avoid discrimination. At the time, many people thought the novel truly was an **autobiography**, because many of the attributes of the main character seemed to fit Johnson as well. In reality, the inspiration for the character came from one of Johnson's friends. The book didn't sell well when it was first published, but it became very popular eight or nine years later, as more people read books by black authors. Johnson later worked for the **NAACP** and published several books of poetry.

Exploring racial themes

Racial identity was often the focus of another author, Jessie Redmon Fauset. Fauset was born in Fredricksville, New Jersey, in 1882. She was well educated, graduating from Cornell University in 1905. Like many other authors at the time, Fauset was an educator before she became known for her writing. She moved to New York City in 1919 and took a job as the **literary editor** of *The Crisis*, a post she held for seven years. Between 1924 and 1931, Fauset wrote three novels, all of which centered on race identity. Later in life, she returned to education.

Fauset's novel *Plum Bun* is about a very light-skinned African-American woman, Angela, who attempts to pass as a white woman in New York City. In order to do this, Angela distances herself from her closest relative, her sister. The novel has a very strong message—that in order to fit into another society, Angela lost touch with her roots. Another of Fauset's novels, *Comedy American Style*, centers on another black woman, but approaches the subject of race in a different way. Like Angela in *Plum Bun*, the character here, Olivia, wants to fit in with white society. In order to accomplish this, Olivia marries a light-skinned black man in an attempt to have very light-skinned children. When one of her children turns out darker than she hopes, she rejects the child and her family falls apart.

Jean Toomer struggled with his racial identity throughout his life, and that served as inspiration for his novels. This is Toomer and his wife, Marjory.

Jean Toomer

Like the subjects of Johnson's *Autobiography* or Fauset's *Plum Bun*, Jean Toomer wrestled with his race and how he fit into society. Toomer was very light-skinned, and many people thought him to be of Mediterranean descent. He struggled with this issue throughout his life. He went back and forth between white and black schools as a youth, and when he married a white woman, other African Americans said he was ignoring his roots. Ironically, *Cane*, his novel about growing up poor and black in Georgia which is now hailed as an example of great literature from the Harlem Renaissance, wasn't popular at the time. It wasn't until the second half of the 20th century that it was mass-produced and widely read.

The Harlem Poets

Despite the prolific numbers of novels and short stories produced by great black writers during the Harlem Renaissance, the era is perhaps best known for its poets. Langston Hughes remains a giant in the world of American poetry. Countee Cullen and Claude McKay are also well known and widely read.

Catching a people's spirit

McKay was born in Jamaica in 1889, but moved to the United States when he was in his early 20s, attending the Tuskegee Institute in Alabama before leaving to study agriculture at Kansas State University. Even before arriving in the United States, McKay tried his hand at poetry, publishing a collection in 1909 called *Songs of Jamaica*, which was written in a Jamaican **dialect**. In 1914, McKay moved to Harlem. At the time, Harlem was still a somewhat hostile environment for blacks. The white residents had dug in their heels and were preparing to fight to keep their neighborhood white. McKay captured the spirit of **hostility** surrounding the black community in a poem published in 1919 called "If We Must Die."

McKay's poem inspired many other writers to pick up their pens and write. He is credited with helping give a start to other poets, such as Langston Hughes.

If We Must Die

by Claude McKay

*If we must die—let it not be like hogs
Hunted and penned in an inglorious spot,
While round us bark the mad and hungry dogs,
Making their mock at our accursed lot.
If we must die—oh, let us nobly die,
So that our precious blood may not be shed
In vain; then even the monsters we defy
Shall be constrained to honor us though dead!*

World-class poet

Langston Hughes first gained widespread recognition for his award-winning poem, "The Weary Blues," but had been published several times before that and was well known in the black community. He was born in 1902 in Joplin, Missouri, and was

> ## Dream Deferred
>
> by Langston Hughes
>
> *What happens to a dream deferred?*
> *Does it dry up*
> *Like a raisin in the sun?*
> *Or fester like a sore—*
> *And then run?*
> *Does it stink like rotten meat?*
> *Or crust and sugar over—*
> *like a syrupy sweet?*
> *Maybe it just sags*
> *like a heavy load.*
> *Or does it explode?*

educated at Columbia University in New York City. It was there that he began submitting work to *The Crisis* for publication. His career took off after his collection of poetry, *The Weary Blues*, was published in 1926. He wrote prolifically for several more decades, including Broadway plays, commentary, and novels.

Hughes is a legendary poet who has transcended time and racial barriers. His most famous work, "Dream Deferred," is read by students around the world, but it wouldn't be fair to categorize Hughes as just a poet. He wrote plays, novels, essays, and children's books. He also was an educator and lecturer.

Countee Cullen

Like Hughes, Countee Cullen had his career launched by winning literary contests. In 1925, at the age of 22, he won several prestigious poetry awards, including *The Crisis* magazine's Amy Spingarn Award. That was also the year that his first book, *Color*, was published. The following year, Cullen began writing a column for *Opportunity* and was named assistant editor of the magazine. He enjoyed a successful writing career before dying at the young age of 42.

*Langston Hughes is one of the most famous writers to come out of the Harlem Renaissance. Hughes was most famous for his poems, but wrote in many different **genres**.*

Musical Theater Makes Harlem Come Alive

American musical theater in the 1910s was mostly performed by white people. The only real outlet for black performers was to put on blackface—make up their faces—and sing humorous songs that usually mocked black people. Noble Sissle and Eubie Blake set out to change that. Sissle was a singer and pianist from Indiana. Blake was also a performer, but concentrated mostly on composing music. He grew up in Maryland. The two first worked together in 1915, writing a song called "It's All Your Fault." The two went their separate ways for a while, and Sissle enlisted in the military.

On to vaudeville

Noble Sissle (left) and Eubie Blake brought serious black theater back to New York with their 1921 musical Shuffle Along.

After the war, the two were planning on working on bringing serious black musical theater back to New York, along with well-known bandleader James Reese Europe. Europe's sudden death put a hold on those plans, however. Sissle and Blake were encouraged to join the white **vaudeville** circuit. They were one of only a handful of African-American acts on the circuit, but they became successful. The two were at an **NAACP** benefit dinner in Philadelphia, Pennsylvania, when they ran across Flournoy Miller and Aubrey Lyles, two other African-American vaudeville performers. The four decided to create and produce a

musical comedy with an all-black cast. The result of their efforts, *Shuffle Along*, opened on the stage of the 63rd Street Theatre in New York on May 23, 1921.

Breaking tradition

Shuffle Along broke several unwritten rules in musical theater. Besides having an all-black cast, the show also featured a love scene between two black people. This had never been done on stage before, and many in the cast feared the worst. They even crowded near a backstage exit, in case the crowd got violent. Instead, the crowd burst into applause after the scene was over. Another change was in the way the audience was seated. Blacks were seated in areas that had previously been white-only areas. Because these areas were generally nicer than the ones that blacks had been forced to sit in before, it was seen as progress, even though the audience was still **segregated**.

The show was a hit, getting good reviews in the press and playing in front of large audiences. This success paved the way for other black musicals to follow. Suddenly, Broadway and other New York theaters were flooded with black musicals. Many of these musicals had songs that became popular hits. "I'm Just Wild About Harry" was a song from *Shuffle Along* that became a hit, and a song from the musical *Runnin' Wild*, started a song and dance craze that swept through the country, known as the Charleston.

Adelaide Hall was one of the stars of Blackbirds of 1928.

A show called *Blackbirds of 1928* opened and was a huge hit—in 1927. The show featured a tap dancer named Bill Robinson, who became better known by his nickname, "Bojangles." The show features several accomplished and talented dancers, including Earl "Snake Hips" Tucker, whose moves would be copied years later by Elvis Presley.

Nightclubs Cater to Downtown Tastes

Jazz music began around the turn of the century, when the **Dixieland** style developed in the New Orleans area. Not long after, jazz became popular in Harlem and the rest of New York. As more southern blacks moved to the city, they brought with them another style of music that became known as the blues. Because it was still unheard of for black musicians to book concert halls, many of these performers got their starts in nightclubs in Harlem.

One of the first such clubs was called Happy Rhone's Black and White Club, and it was located on the corner of 143rd Street and Lenox Avenue. This club, run by Arthur "Happy" Rhone, was ahead of its time. It was one of the first clubs to have waitresses and floorshows. And it was **integrated**.

Whites only

Most nightclubs during this time were **segregated**. African Americans were only allowed in the clubs to perform, wash dishes, or check coats. Blacks in Harlem couldn't go watch their friends perform—they'd have to sit outside and listen. In one particularly ironic incident, a blues composer named W. C. Handy wasn't allowed in a club—even though the musicians inside were playing a song that he had written.

These nightclubs also often played to ethnic and cultural **stereotypes**. Even though most performers were born in the United States—many of them just a few blocks from the clubs themselves—the clubs reinforced the connection between the performers and Africa. Exotic jungle decorations were meant to make the white audience feel as though they were in a different place. In addition, almost all Harlem nightclubs sold beer and liquor, even though these were outlawed by the 18th Amendment in 1919. This added to the clubs' dangerous and exotic feel.

The Cotton Club

The Cotton Club was the most famous nightclub in Harlem; in fact, it is still well known today. Like most other clubs at the time, it was whites-only. The Cotton Club was just a block away from Happy Rhone's, on the corner of 142nd and Lenox, and was probably the most popular club in Harlem. Nearly 700 people filled the club every night to see elaborate shows with chorus girls and the famous band led by Duke Ellington.

Another popular club was the Savoy Ballroom. This massive building occupied a whole block, from 140th Street to 141st Street. The club featured Fletcher Henderson and the Rainbow Orchestra. It was one of the first large groups to play jazz. The orchestra drew crowds to the ballroom, and got its own radio show broadcast from the building. People were captivated by the new style, the beginning of big band. One of the hit songs of the time was "Stompin' at the Savoy," a tribute to the ballroom and its band.

Countless legendary musicians passed through the doorways of Harlem's jazz and blues clubs during the Harlem Renaissance. Duke Ellington, Louis Armstrong, Jelly Roll Morton, Bessie Smith, Billie Holiday, Josephine Baker, Ella Fitzgerald, and many others performed at Harlem's famous clubs.

The Cotton Club is one of the most famous clubs in Harlem. Almost every important jazz or blues musician played there at some point during their career.

The Apollo Theatre

One of Harlem's most famous landmarks is the historic Apollo Theatre. The Apollo is probably the best-known African-American theater in the world. Some of the world's most famous performers got their start there. During the time of the Harlem Renaissance, the building, then known as Seamon's Music Hall, was a concert hall that featured mostly white **vaudeville** acts for a mostly white crowd. It wasn't until the 1930s that the theater was renamed and became a home for African-American acts like Duke Ellington, Ella Fitzgerald, Sarah Vaughn, Count Basie, and, later, James Brown, Stevie Wonder, and the Jackson Five.

The Harlem Renaissance Painters

Aaron Douglas began painting in a classical style. After he moved to New York, he became known for his cubist murals.

Like so many African-American authors who were moved to write about living as a black person, so too did African-American artists depict scenes of black life. Harlem called to black artists, and people like Aaron Douglas, Palmer Hayden, and William H. Johnson arrived.

A folk influence

Aaron Douglas was born in Topeka, Kansas, in 1899. He was interested in art from a young age, and graduated from the University of Nebraska with a degree in Fine Arts in 1922. Like many others who later moved to Harlem, Douglas started his career in education, teaching art at a high school in Topeka for two years. In 1924, Douglas went to Harlem, drawn by the **cultural revolution** that was taking place at the time. In Harlem he met Winold Reiss, a German painter. Even though they came from very different backgrounds, Reiss helped Douglas and influenced his paintings. Reiss had been using folk characters in his art for years, and encouraged Douglas to do the same. Douglas moved away from his **classical** European training and painted black figures. He used something of a **cubist** style in many of his paintings. During the late 1920s, Douglas became very popular and was commissioned to paint murals around the country, including at the Harlem branch of the New York Public Library.

Painting the working class

Palmer Hayden was also a trained painter, but had a very different style than Douglas. He was born Peyton Hedgeman, but was given the name Palmer Hayden by his commanding sergeant in World War I.

Hayden was born in Wide Water, Virginia, in 1890. He studied at two different schools and moved to New York in 1919. Like Douglas, Hayden was one of the first formally trained black artists to paint black subjects. However, their styles were very different. Where Douglas painted in a cubist style, most of Hayden's paintings are more classical in nature. Early in his career, Hayden received a lot of criticism. Some people said that his paintings were racist because they portrayed the black lower class. Many felt that he exaggerated and added to the **stereotypes** of black Americans. Eventually though, critics recognized his work as groundbreaking.

Palmer Hayden painted in a classical style. This painting, "New York City Hall," is of the old city hall building in New York City.

A contrast in styles

William H. Johnson arrived in Harlem in 1918 from Florence, South Carolina. He was quite young at the time, having been born in 1901. He traveled to New York to become a student at the National Academy of Design. During his first few years in New York, Johnson painted with a classical style, but his art changed at the end of the 1920s. Instead of using the muted colors and long strokes of classical and **expressionist** painters, Johnson began using bright colors and contrasts and painting in two dimensions. He called it a "primitive" style of painting. Johnson's style would later influence other great American artists, such as Jacob Lawrence, who became famous for painting black figures using bright and contrasting colors.

These three artists were among the very first Americans to portray blacks in art. Their contrasts in styles and backgrounds create a very different body of work for each of them, but all influenced later African-American artists.

Portraits of the Visual Artists

Painters were a large part of the Harlem Renaissance, but artists in other media also thrived and gained recognition. Illustrators, sculptors, and photographers became well known and respected. Augusta Savage, Meta Fuller, and James Van Der Zee were just a few of the visual artists that contributed to the culture of the time.

Augusta Savage moved to New York with less than five dollars. A few years later, she was making sculptures of some of the most famous people in the city.

An American sculptor

Augusta Savage was born in Green Cove Springs, Florida, in 1892. In 1907, her family moved to West Palm Beach. Savage enrolled in art classes, and taught at the same time to make money on the side. She tried to make a living by sculpting **busts** of the black elite in Jacksonville, Florida, but was unsuccessful. In 1920, Savage moved to New York with $4.60. She began taking art courses at Cooper Union in

1921, enrolling in a four-year sculpture program. After seeing her work, her instructors advanced her past the first two years. Savage wanted to study in Europe, and in 1923, she was selected to study in France as part of a group of 100 young American women. When the French realized that Savage was black, her invitation was cancelled. It wasn't until the late 1920s that Savage finally got the chance to go to Europe. In the mid 1920s, she was commissioned to make busts of W. E. B. DuBois and Marcus Garvey. Both statues won critical acclaim. Later in life, she became an art educator in Harlem. Most of Savage's work was done in clay and plaster that has since been destroyed. Only a few of her pieces survive today.

Sculpture in action

Meta Fuller was also a sculptor. While Savage mostly did busts, Fuller's sculptures portrayed blacks doing things. She was born in Philadelphia in 1877 and studied at several art schools and in Paris. Her sculptures are of a very **classical** design, influenced by her studies in Paris. Fuller was one of the first American artists to use black subjects in her work. She did so as early as the first few years of the 20th century, well before the Harlem Renaissance. While Fuller never lived in Harlem, her work and innovation was a major influence on the artists of the Harlem Renaissance.

Documenting history

James Van Der Zee was a photographer who documented life in Harlem over a period of several decades. Van Der Zee was born in Lenox, Massachusetts, in 1886. He won a camera when he was 12 years old and experimented with it, but only as a hobby—his chosen profession was music. He moved to Harlem in 1906 and formed the Harlem Orchestra. His musical career was mildly successful, but by 1915, he was having trouble finding work as a musician. He took a job as a darkroom technician, but found himself standing in as a photographer from time to time. He enjoyed it and opened his own studio in 1917. Over the course of the next 60 years or so, he captured nearly every aspect of life in Harlem: weddings, funerals, parades, athletic events, people in the street, people in nightclubs, family portraits, street scenes. Unknown to the outside world, Van Der Zee documented almost every conceivable event, place, and object in Harlem. It wasn't until 1968 that Van Der Zee's work was discovered by a photo researcher named Reginald McGhee. McGhee found more than 75,000 of Van Der Zee's photos. The following year, the Metropolitan Museum of Art exhibited many of them and Van Der Zee became famous. He continued taking photos until his death in 1983.

James Van Der Zee worked in anonymity for decades before his photographs were discovered in the 1960s. Van Der Zee documented life in Harlem, such as this photograph of a couple from 1932.

The Women of the Harlem Renaissance

Even though Harlem was seen as a refuge from the racism and harsh realities of being black in the United States during the 1910s and 1920s, things weren't perfect there. Life for women during this time was also difficult. Most of society still believed that men were superior to women. Educational and business opportunities for women were few and far between. Being black and female was a huge burden when trying to break into a white, male-dominated society. Despite these challenges, women were an integral part of the Harlem Renaissance.

Voice of the South

Zora Neale Hurston was born in Alabama in 1891. She attended high school in Baltimore and enrolled at Howard University, a black university in Washington, D.C., in 1919. She studied on and off at Howard for several years. Hurston was very interested in poetry, and studied under Georgia Douglas Johnson, a well known poet at the time. She also met editor Alain Locke, who was teaching philosophy. Hurston published her first story in 1921, in a Howard campus magazine. Her story caught the attention of Charles S. Johnson in Harlem, and he encouraged her to move to New York to pursue a career in writing. She moved to Harlem in 1925 and won her *Opportunity* awards just a few months later. Hurston's successful beginning led to an impressive career. She wrote several novels and short stories, and is best known for her 1937 novel, *Their Eyes Were Watching God*.

A prolific artist

Gwendolyn Bennett was born in Texas in 1902. When Bennett was young, her family moved several times around the country. They finally settled in Brooklyn and Gwendolyn attended high school there. She was very interested in the arts and writing while in school. She was involved in school literary and drama societies, and won first place in an art contest. After graduating in 1921, Bennett enrolled in fine arts studies at Columbia University. Later, she transferred to the Pratt Institute, and graduated in 1924.

In 1923, *The Crisis* ran one of Bennett's illustrations for its cover. The same year, one of her poems, "Heritage," was published in *Opportunity*. Over the next several years, dozens of her poems were published in various magazines and journals. Despite Bennett's early success, she did not devote her life to her own writing. Rather, she joined many boards and guilds to help other young people learn to write and display their talents.

Black or white?

Nella Larsen was born as Nellie Walker in Chicago in 1891. Her childhood was filled with racial confusion. Historians think her father changed his name from Peter Walker to Peter Larsen in order to pass as white and take a job with a railroad. Her own mother didn't want to have an obviously black child and separated herself from Nella for most of her life. Larsen trained as a nurse and, in 1916, moved to New York City to take a nursing job. She became well connected in the arts movement at the time, and eventually took a job in the Harlem branch of the New York Public Library. She improved her writing skills and published several short stories in the mid 1920s. Her first novel, *Quicksand*, was published in 1928 and was a success. Larsen wrote for a few more years before she stopped writing for publication and lived out the rest of her life as a nurse in Brooklyn.

Nella Larsen was born in Chicago, but moved to Harlem in the early stages of the Renaissance. She worked at the Harlem branch of the New York Public Library, and published several books. Here she receives a Harman Award.

Gender issues

Marita Bonner was born in 1899 in a suburb of Boston. She attended Radcliffe College in Massachusetts, and studied English and literature. After graduation, she taught in public schools for many years, while writing on the side. Bonner wrote several short stories and essays that talked not only about the difficulties of being black in the 1920s, but of being a black woman then. In 1925 she wrote an autobiographical essay for *The Crisis* called "On Being Young, a Woman, and Colored." During the late 1920s, several more of her stories, essays, and plays were published. In 1930, she married and moved to Chicago, where she continued to teach and write until her death in 1971.

The Patrons of the Arts

Artists and writers who are just beginning their careers often don't make enough money to live on their work alone. That was the case with most of the creative talent during the Harlem Renaissance. Only a few artists and writers were able to make enough money to be **self-sufficient** early on in their careers. Talented people will often have **patrons**, who help support them in order to enjoy their work. The writers, artists, and musicians of the Harlem Renaissance had many different patrons, but three of the biggest were Carl Van Vechten, Charlotte Osgood Mason, and A'Lelia Walker.

An unlikely patron

Carl Van Vechten was a white man who took an odd route to becoming a patron of the black arts. He was born in Cedar Rapids, Iowa, in 1880 and studied at the prestigious University of Chicago. Later, he moved to New York City and became a music critic. It was then that he took notice of the Harlem Renaissance movement. He became friends with writer James Weldon Johnson and actor Paul Robeson, but his most public friendship was with poet Langston Hughes. Van Vechten, being in the white publishing world, had many contacts and friends in the business. He served as a matchmaker of sorts, setting up talented black writers with eager white publishers. Later, he became a novelist and photographer, writing the book *Nigger Heaven*. The book's name made it controversial, but critics and the public that actually read *Nigger Heaven* praised it.

Controversial views

Charlotte Osgood Mason was a wealthy white widow who had an interest in black writers and poetry. She met Langston Hughes through Alain Locke, and was immediately taken with the young poet. Hughes was similarly impressed with Mason, who wanted to support him financially. Mason believed that blacks were "primitive people" who were close with nature and produced "natural" art. She said she wanted

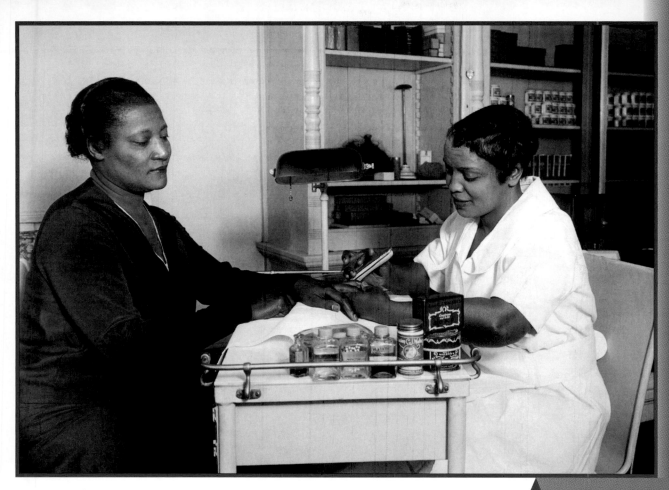

to save these works, and that was her motivation for helping. Later, she would also sponsor writer Zora Neale Hurston and painter Aaron Douglas. Eventually, all three had a falling out with Mason, and her support ended.

Heiress to a fortune

A'Lelia Walker, the daughter of millionaire Madam C. J. Walker, inherited her mother's estate and wealth when she died in 1919. A'Lelia was born in Vicksburg, Mississippi, in 1885 and worked for her mother's company for years. When she was just 23, A'Lelia was running the company's Pittsburgh office and a **cosmetology** school named for her. A'Lelia became a **philanthropist** in the tradition of her mother, giving money to local and national organizations. She also hosted parties where the black arts community met with white editors, publishers, and patrons. She held massive and elaborate parties at her Harlem townhome, which she named "The Dark Tower." Countee Cullen, Langston Hughes, Zora Neale Hurston, James Weldon Johnson, and Jean Toomer were all regular guests of Walker. Walker was sometimes the target of criticism, as some blacks felt that she was exploiting African-American writing and art just to show off to her white friends, but the fact remains that she was one of the largest patrons of the time.

A'Lelia Walker (left) inherited her mother's company and money after her death in 1919. A'Lelia became an important patron of the arts in Harlem, giving money to all kinds of groups, writers, and artists.

In Whose Voice?

It is easy to look at everything produced during the Harlem Renaissance as one large body of work. In truth, the writers, painters, and musicians produced work that was just as different then as writers, painters, and musicians produce today.

Leading the fight

W. E. B. DuBois believed and wrote strongly about the need for African Americans to strive to be the best they could. He urged blacks to fight for their rights in the legal and court systems, to live honorable lives, and to claim what was theirs. His essays were impassioned and direct, and his fiction work wasn't much different. In fact, some of his fiction might be considered heavy-handed by today's standards—much of it focused on showing that blacks were just as talented and intelligent as whites. While that may seem obvious to readers now, for some of DuBois' audience, it was thought-provoking and revolutionary.

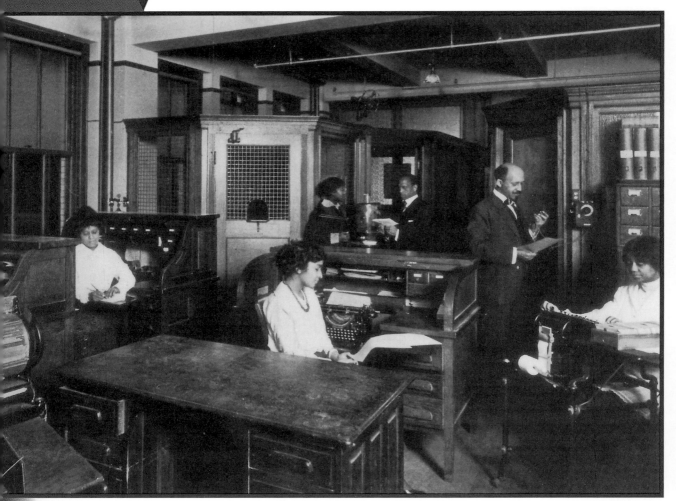

Contrasting views

Of course, there were **dissenters** then—people who made the argument that blacks were naturally inferior to whites—just as there are now. Sometimes, some of the most insulting views came from people who were sympathetic to the plight of African Americans. Patron Charlotte Osgood Mason is one example. Her methods were almost diametrically opposite to those of activists like DuBois. Instead of encouraging blacks to take their places alongside whites, Mason believed that African Americans needed to have their art and writing preserved as an example of something natural and pure.

Really, most writers didn't get involved with racial discussions on this level. While some, such as DuBois and Charles S. Johnson, used their pens for political statements, most used them simply to tell good stories. James Weldon Johnson's book, *The Autobiography of an Ex-Colored Man*, certainly had racial undertones—and may have even been primarily about race—but was a story more than anything else. The same could be said for Jessie Fauset's novels and some of Countee Cullen's poems. Although race was often a central topic, and some of the works had moralistic overtones, they were not directly addressing issues the way that a DuBois essay would. Other writers didn't mention race much. Zora Neale Hurston wrote about African Americans, but much of her work doesn't discuss race or racial issues at all.

The sum collection of all of these works is an incredible resource, not only to show how African Americans lived in Harlem in the 1910s and 1920s, but also to show the lives and stories of individual African Americans living at this time.

Jessie Redmon Fauset focused on race in her stories. In her most famous work, the main character tries to hide her racial background from society and shuns her family to do so.

The Harlem Renaissance Comes to an End

The Harlem Renaissance began gradually as the culmination of several social and economic forces in a New York City neighborhood. It did not end nearly as gradually. In late 1928 and early 1929, some people were getting worried about the country's economy. No one expected what happened in October 1929. On October 24, 1929, the **stock market**, which had been rising for years, fell significantly. Just five days later, the bottom fell out of the market on what came to be known as Black Tuesday. The crash was the first in a chain of events that led to the **Great Depression**. In just under three years, U.S. stocks lost 89 percent of their value. Many companies went bankrupt. Most of those that were left were barely getting by, and few companies turned a profit. The result was that many people lost their jobs. The people that kept jobs often did so while taking pay cuts.

Millions of people lost their jobs during the Great Depression. New York City was hit especially hard. Here, two unemployed men pose in Harlem in 1936.

Money dries up

Suddenly, people who had been very wealthy had little money—some were even in debt. Even those who had secure investments and held on to their money were suddenly a lot less likely to spend it. Jobs disappeared instantly and the **unemployment rate** went sky high. Many blacks had it worse than the population at large. Blacks were usually among the first to get fired or laid off. In neighborhoods like Harlem, the effect was devastating. Suddenly a large portion of the workforce was unemployed and had no disposable income. That hurt the restaurants, clubs, stores, barbershops, and other businesses in neighborhoods like Harlem. Many of those businesses failed, putting more people on the street. In a little more than a year, the unemployment rate in Harlem jumped to 50 percent.

A helping hand

The people of Harlem tried to help their neighbors. Churches and social organizations like the **National Urban League** worked to supply people with clothes, shelter, and food. They helped to find

people work, even if it was only for a day or two. For people who relied on others' **discretionary spending** for income—like writers, artists, and musicians—the audience suddenly dried up. No one had the money to purchase magazines or books or paintings or go to clubs. Some got by for a while through support of **patrons** such as Charlotte Osgood Mason and A'Lelia Walker, but that eventually ended, too.

Moving on

Many of the key figures in the Harlem Renaissance took positions in education. Charles S. Johnson, James Weldon Johnson, and Aaron Douglas all took positions at Fisk University in the late 1920s to late 1930s. Countee Cullen taught English and French at a New York City junior high school. Education offered job security, good pay and benefits, and the opportunity to teach to the next generation of poets, artists, and authors. Others, such as Langston Hughes and Palmer Hayden, traveled around the world to places less affected by the American economy. In many cases, writers stopped writing and painters stopped painting.

By the time that A'Lelia Walker died in 1931, the Harlem Renaissance was all but over. The money had dried up, and, to many people, social causes and the arts weren't as important as surviving the Great Depression. Many wealthy people didn't want to spend money on luxuries like music and writing during a time of financial uncertainty. Many of the key players left Harlem and never looked back.

Although the Great Depression signaled the end of the Harlem Renaissance, it wasn't the end of the arts in Harlem. In 1937, the first all-black ballet and all-black orchestra premiered at the Lafayette Theater in Harlem.

The Harlem Renaissance Legacy

Today the Harlem Renaissance stands as an era in which African Americans made enormous progress in exposing their art and culture to the rest of the world. For the first time in the history of America, the work of its black citizens was respected on a wide scale.

Another Renaissance?

After A'Lelia Walker's death, things got worse for Harlem. The economy continued to do poorly and in 1935 a large riot in the neighborhood caused more than $2 million worth of damage. The **Great Depression** and the riots took a toll on Harlem. It became a less desirable place to live and had a national reputation as such. Many of its upper- and middle-income residents left for the suburbs. More riots in the 1960s solidified that reputation, and Harlem seemed destined to become an urban wasteland.

But by the end of the 20th century, things had changed for the better. Businesses moved back into Harlem, crime went down, old buildings were renovated and middle- and upper-class residents began moving back to the area.

Around the turn of the 21st century, many businesses relocated to Harlem. The former President of the United States, Bill Clinton, chose Harlem as the location for his office when he left the White House in 2001. Here, he meets local people outside his new office.

The concentration of talent in two square miles of New York City fostered an attitude of cultural appreciation and growth. While many of the major players were educated and well-read, it is unlikely that many of them grew up reading a large amount of black literature—until that time, little of it existed. Living and working in a place where black literature was in the bookstores, magazines, and newspapers could only have helped inspire more people to pick up their pens. Seeing paintings, sketches, and photographs of Harlem's people undoubtedly pushed others to seek cameras, canvasses, and chalks.

The influence of the era on the present is enormous. The **NAACP** and **National Urban League** are still influential, powerful organizations working for black citizens. The handful of magazines such as *The Crisis* and *Opportunity* have given birth to dozens of periodicals aimed at an African-American audience. The pioneer authors, poets, and writers paved the way for today's stars in those fields. African-American music has never been as popular as it is today, and other media, like **Black Entertainment Television**, have expanded on the foundation that was laid in Harlem in the 1910s and 20s.

Many of the works of the time are still recognized as being extraordinary today, not only because they were the first, but also because they were good. For the first time in American history, a segment of the population found its voice and used it to tell stories—in clay, in poetry, and in song.

Lift Every Voice and Sing

Lyrics to James Weldon Johnson's hymn, "Lift Every Voice and Sing." Known as the "Negro National Anthem," this song is so popular in the black community that entire books have been written about it.

Lift every voice and sing
Till earth and heaven ring,
Ring with the harmonies of Liberty;
Let our rejoicing rise
High as the listening skies,
Let it resound loud as the rolling sea.
Sing a song full of the faith that the dark past has taught us,
Sing a song full of the hope that the present has brought us;
Facing the rising sun of our new day begun
Let us march on till victory is won.

Harlem Renaissance Timeline

1658	A Dutch settlement named Nieuw Haarlem is established.
1664	English take over the Dutch settlements in the area. Nieuw Haarlem is renamed Harlem.
1873	New York City annexes Harlem.
1904	New York City subway reaches Harlem, making it more accessible than ever before.
1909	The National Association for the Advancement of Colored People (NAACP) organizes in Illinois.
1910	The Committee on Urban Conditions Among Negroes (later the National Urban League) is formed in New York City and spreads to other cities. The NAACP publishes the first issue of *The Crisis*.
1911	St. Philip's Episcopal Church, the biggest black church in New York, moves to Harlem, builds a new church and buys homes in the area.
1912	James Weldon Johnson's book *The Autobiography of an Ex-Colored Man* is published.
1916	Madam C. J. Walker, the first self-made American female millionaire, moves to Harlem to join her daughter, A'Lelia. Marcus Garvey and his UNIA organization also move to Harlem.
1917	Race riots in East St. Louis, Illinois.
1919	Race riots in several cities across the United States. NAACP pushes legislators to deal with lynchings.
1920	Marcus Garvey and the UNIA hold the First International Convention of the Negro Peoples of the World in Madison Square Garden.
1921	*Shuffle Along,* a musical written by Eubie Blake and Noble Sissle, opens at the 63rd Street Theatre.
1922	Meta Fuller's sculpture is part of an exhibit in New York called Making of America.
1923	The National Urban League publishes the first issue of *Opportunity: A Journal of Negro Life.* Jean Toomer's novel *Cane* is published.
1924	Charles S. Johnson holds the Civic Club Dinner to introduce talented blacks to well-connected whites. Aaron Douglas moves to Harlem.
1925	*Survey Graphic* magazine publishes its "The New Negro" issue, edited by Alain Locke. *Opportunity* and *The Crisis* hold their literary awards dinners.
1926	Langston Hughes publishes his first book of poetry, *The Weary Blues*. The Savoy Ballroom opens with Fletcher Henderson and his orchestra.
1927	Duke Ellington performs at the Cotton Club.
1929	Stock market crashes, beginning the end of the Harlem Renaissance.
1931	A'Lelia Walker dies at age 46. Less money is available for artists and writers. End of the Harlem Renaissance.

Further Reading

Chambers, Veronica. *The Harlem Renaissance.* Broomhall, Pa.: Chelsea House Publishers, 1997.

Gaines, Ann Graham. *The Harlem Renaissance in American History.* Berkeley Heights, N.J.: Enslow Publishers, Inc., 2002.

Hardy, P. Stephan and Sheila Jackson. *Extraordinary People of the Harlem Renaissance.* Danbury, Conn.: Scholastic Library Publishing, 2000.

Kallen, Stuart A. *The Harlem Renaissance.* Minneapolis, Minn.: ABDO Publishing Co., 2001.

Locke, Alain, ed. *The New Negro.* New York, N.Y.: Simon & Schuster Trade, 1999.

Glossary

agenda program of things to be done, or the goals of a group of people

agents people who sell a business's products

annex to add a tract of land to a governmental body

autobiography the story of a person's life, told by that person

bachelor's degree qualification given by a college or university to a person who has completed a group of courses

Black Entertainment Television (BET) cable channel delivering news and entertainment for and about African Americans

busts sculptures of a person's head and shoulders

civil rights individual rights that all members of a society have to freedom and equal treatment under the law

classical traditional or accepted course of study

cosmetology skill of using and applying cosmetics, usually in a beauty shop or salon

cubist movement in art, mostly in the early 20th century, characterized by the use of cubes and other geometric forms when portraying a subject

cultural revolution bringing a new culture forward suddenly

dialect form of speech used in a particular district

discretionary spending spending money by choice instead of by necessity

discrimination prejudice or unjust behavior to others based on differences in age, race, gender, etc.

dissenters people who disagree with an opinion

Dixieland style of jazz music that began in New Orleans, featuring small groups playing together and solo improvisation

editorials articles or statements that reflect an opinion in newspapers or magazines

entrepreneurs people who start their own businesses and are good at finding new ways to make money

expressionist describes an art movement that used symbols and other abstract figures to portray emotions

genre kind, or type, of literature or art

Great Depression a time when businesses and trade collapsed, causing job losses. It began in 1929 and continued through the 1930s.

hostility unfriendliness, hatred, or opposition

integrated something that includes all races

Jim Crow laws laws, especially found in the Southern United States during the early 20th century, that prevented blacks from voting and practicing other civil rights

Ku Klux Klan secret society of white men that practices discrimination against minorities

legacy something handed down from one generation to another

legislators people who work at making and voting on laws

literary editor someone who prepares other people's stories, essays, plays, or poems for publication

lynching the murder of a person by a group of people. Lynchings of blacks by whites were widespread in the United States in the early 20th century.

mortgage loan from a bank to buy a house or property

NAACP National Association for the Advancement of Colored People civil rights group started in 1909 after a race riot in Illinois.

National Urban League organization that was started in 1910 to help Southern blacks move to the North

Pan-African Congress meeting between black leaders from around the world

patron someone who gives money to or helps another person, an activity, or a cause

philanthropist person who helps others by giving time or money to causes and charities

race riots violence and fighting in a community, brought on by racial conflicts and hatred

radical holding extreme opinions, usually involving political change

realtor person who helps others buy and sell homes

segregated describes people kept apart based on race, gender, or other factors

segregation act of keeping people or groups apart

self-made millionaire person who makes a million dollars (or more) by working, instead of inheriting it

self-sufficient having the necessary resources to get along without help

slum usually heavily populated area of a city, characterized by poverty, poor housing and substandard education

sociology study of the ways in which people live together in different societies

stereotype overly simple picture or opinion of a person, group, or thing

stock market place where stocks are bought and sold

tenement house run-down apartment building, especially one that is crowded and in a poor part of a city

unemployment rate the percentage of people without jobs

UNIA Universal Negro Improvement Association. The organization that Marcus Garvey started that moved from Jamaica to Harlem in 1916.

vaudeville kind of musical theater consisting of several performing acts such as singers, dancers, comedians, acrobats, etc.

Walloons French-speaking people from southern Belgium

Index